Mokie
THE
Bear

A story of Friendship

RON AMAREL

A Story of Friendship

This book is dedicated to my grandchildren. I wanted them to know this story first hand, just as their mothers were told. This is a story that was created during a long road trip on Easter many years ago. One of those trips when the radio is turned down and the parents (OK mostly Dad) is going to start talking.

Because we lived a distance from our family, we made many of these trips with stories, questions and opinions shared to reduce the fatigue of the miles.

I want to thank my wife, Lynette and my 4 daughters, Rebecca, Terra, Carrie and Ashlie for putting up with my stories as this is only one example, but one that has remained in our thoughts every Easter after that.

God put us here to be someone.
To be someone you have to do something.
To do something you have to help someone.
And pray that the chain never breaks

Mokie with a caring heart as big as a bear!

Ron Amarel

It was a very nice, early Easter morning.
The grass was green, the flowers were blooming.
The colors of the hillside were bright and stunning.

Coming down from the hill was the Easter Bunny, not hopping but limping.

It stopped and sat next to one of the trees and fell asleep.

Dreaming of its tasks and undone deeds.

"Knowing all the eggs and candy, I have to share.
There are still a few minutes that I can spare."

The bunny heard a noise coming from the hill.
It was loud and clear as the wind was still.

A bear, in a slow and sure style, stepped up to the bunny.

"It is a great day, beautiful and sunny
Good morning, hop-along you look kind of funny.
What is the problem, is the question fair?
I am Mokie...............Mokie the Bear.
I did not want to scare you by wakening you this way.
But, willing to listen. What do you have to say?"

"I am the Easter Bunny and have things to do.
Easter may not be the same this year.
And in my condition……….. that I fear".

"We believe in the day and for the kids we both care.
I'm sure I can help, with ideas and I'm willing to share."

"My foot is sore and I cannot get anything done this way.
I stopped at a nearby farm, searching for someone willing to help me this day."

"The pig was willing, but would eat all himself.
The cow was interested, but stayed on the felt."

"Willing to help was a little red hen.
She wanted to keep a lot for herself
And stayed in the pen."

"There was a goose, that did not seem too golden.
The farmer, but with too many chores beholden.
I stopped to think, there is no interest here.
I have to get going, but my sore foot I fear."

Mokie asked the Easter Bunny to see its foot
Found a "goat head" sticker
In between the toes, it was put.
Mokie started to laugh and thought it was funny,
Picturing a goat head, on a bunny.

Mokie told the bunny,
"Keep positive thoughts in your brain.
With my paw and a flicker
I will remove the pain"

"I know a few that may be able to help."
Then Mokie stopped with caution
And gave it more thought.
"My family, but they are all bears.
A bear, not a bunny,
I'm sure will cause stares."

"There are other animals, in the forest they feed.
I'm sure willing to help if they knew the Easter Bunny was in need."

"But your foot is better so let's get going
Let's start the eggs and candy a flowing"

Mokie was pleased to see The Easter Bunny a hoppin.

Eggs and candy were provided to all, no one forgotten.
A lot of hard work, but a great pleasure we feel.
Many can benefit when a good deed becomes real.

Together we got a lot of things done.
Working together, hard work became fun.

What a great day!
A good deed that brought a lot of fun and pleasure.

A new friend, one I will have forever

Friends and family, those you will never forget.
Others are friends we do not know well enough yet.

Just like an Easter Egg we are not the same.
But working together we can do anything.

It was a great friendship that was born that day.
The first Sunday after the first full moon,
We call Easter Sunday.

When we celebrate Easter, candy and eggs you can find.
Let's not forget the blessings of our family and Jesus,
His love for Man Kind.